Pick Up a Shell

By Liza Charlesworth

ISBN: 978-1-339-02771-5

Art Director: Tannaz Fassihi; Designer: Tanya Chernyak
Photos © Getty Images and Shutterstock.com.
Copyright © Liza Charlesworth. All rights reserved. Published by Scholastic Inc.

1 2 3 4 5 6 7 8 9 10   68   32 31 30 29 28 27 26 25 24 23

Printed in Jiaxing, China. First printing, August 2023.

■SCHOLASTIC

Sit in the sand!
You can see a ship.
You can see a shell.

This shell is shut.
It has a clam in it.
A shell is a clam's home.

Rush, rush!
A crab gets in a shell.
The crab has a home.

Swish, swish!
A fish swims in a shell.
The fish can rest in it.

Shells, shells, shells!
Shops sell shells and get cash.
Shells can be a lot of shapes.

A shell can be black or pink.
A shell can be tan with spots.

Pick up a shell.
Shhhhhhhhhhhh.
It has the sea in it!